WHAT EVERYONE SHOULD KNOW ABOUT

LORETTA

Loretta Knapp

ISBN: 978-1-4669-3030-8 (sc)
ISBN: 978-1-4669-3031-5 (e)

Trafford rev. 05/07/2012

 www.trafford.com

North America & international
toll-free: 1 888 232 4444 (USA & Canada)
phone: 250 383 6864 ♦ fax: 812 355 4082

Contents

What Is Love?

Have you ever stop to think, What is love? I often wonder what love is really about. People aren't showing any love, and what love they do show only last maybe two or three weeks. Remember when you were in 2nd grade and your teacher told you the Ten Commandments, which stated love one another? I haven't seen many people loving one another. I hear people bragging how rich they are, but do you think they'd give at least $5.00 to a very poor person? No. We all stand back and watch the person walk down the street with torn up clothes and no shoes and we laugh how he struggles through life. One other thing people do out of ignorance is gossip about how people act. I mean their friends always have money to go places, act so big because they have a lot of money and you don't. This world is getting disgusting, and there's definitely no Love. Jesus is the only one who showed us what Love is. He showed his Love by dying for us. I once thought love started out with two people, a girl and a boy. The first step is to get married. The one reason they get married is that the couple feel they love one another and now they are living together, and it gets rougher each day for both of them. So one day the couple sits down and have a talk. The next thing you know, they are getting a divorce and the reason is that, they're just like me. They don't know what Love is, but the couple don't stop to think of love. I'm at least trying to figure out what love is. Love is beginning to leave us, and hate is taking over the world. In my own opinion, love is something special. Love can come in all colors, shapes, sizes. This world have to shape up and bring back love. Let love start the day first with your family and with all your relatives. Please bring back love, and show it for others, people who don't know what love is. Before you get married, stop and think, do we really love each other or has love definitely grown on me? When you stop and think of all that, I said you are ready to begin a new life. Sometime and somewhere we will all find out what Love is and where it begins.

What Is Love?

What is Love and where is Love.
Does It begin you or does it begin with me.
There are two kinds of Love don't you see.
Now tell me which Love is really me.
Can you see love or can you touch love.
I wish I knew, don't you.
So very few know about love when the whole world should know about it.
Cant you see love trying to grow in me?

The Meaning of Friendship

What does it mean to be a friend.
A helping hand to a journey end.
A loyal heart and a loving one too,
No task to great for a friend to do.

What does it mean to be a friend.
A burden carried around the bends
A hill to climb for another's sake.
There's nothing a friend wont undertake.

What does it mean to be a friend.
A tongue that is quickest to defend.
A friend comes through when the test demands
A friend is a person who understands.

What does it take to be friend.
A life to keep a purpose to lend.
A sort of friend I want to be
The kind of friend you are to me.

We Pass This Way But Once

We walk this good, good green earth but once
We have but one chance to live
In a kindly way as we pass along
There is but one chance to give.

There is only one chance to smile a smile
To hold out your hand to a brother
Such a very short time to work at the art
On sharing with one another.

One little life time—the days are few
That it seems such a waste of time
To find fault with neighbors or pick at our friends
Who seem to step out of line.

The earth is so full of goodness of God
And the blessings of life are so vast
Why do we stop to look back with regret
At mistakes all in the past.

Loretta Knapp

Every new day is a chance to see
The best that's there is on life's way
And each setting sun brings the time to reflect
I've done what I could for today.

What Christmas Means

Stop one minute and think hard about it, now do you know what to say? Christmas is supposed to be a joyous time. It's when we start preparing for the coming of the Savior baby Jesus Christ and they spread the glorious word that Mary had given birth to a baby boy and he laid in a manger and his name shall be called Jesus. And then people began to travel and the Three Kings brought gifts. The day the miracle happened was on December 25th in the town of Bethlehem.

We celebrate Christmas by going shopping for gifts for the loved ones, the children, and friends.

We also celebrate Christmas Eve by having a dinner and go to midnight mass to share the good news. Families gathered around the Christmas tree and give presents to one another. It shouldn't matter the size or the price, it's the thought that counts, is what it means to me.

Christmas, Santa Claus comes and you have to leave him milk and cookies out so you can receive a gift. But you have to make sure you were a good little girl or boy. Spread the glorious word that the Christ child is born . . . Alleluia and Merry Christmas.

What Do I Expect
Out of Life

Well its like this, I only wanted to be loved and accepted in this bad world. And be my own person. There are days when maybe I expect to much of myself. I sometimes put the blame on me. I want to be treated as an individual and not in competition between my family members or my friends.

Back in 1998, when you were punished, especially when you were told no! They meant it. And then when you behaved, you received a reward of food, and then I was told don't eat too much. I'm getting fat. I didn't understand which way to turn. I feel I did live by Mrs. Knapp's rules, and where did it get me.

I ended up seeking counseling and seeing a doctor. I'm scared for life. I expect to much from my own self, and got disappointed because I think my mom wont like me or respect me, she does it to me now. Why should things change now?

I just need my self esteem lifted up, it can be a good thing, its not easy. Problems can be solved without leading to suicide.

In Remembrance of Ruth Heffley

My Friend Ruth

As I take journey down this long and windy road, I recall the memories we share together. You had a birthday party at your house for my sister and I when we were little.

But there was something about you I knew I could trust you. So, as I got older I placed my trust in you and would call and you would come down and pick me up and take me for ice cream and we would have our talk.

I got lonely and miss our talks. I remember even when you were battling cancer and I got in trouble and you took me in, and I slept over night and you were still working. You took me school.

After I graduated we would meet at McDonalds for coffee sometimes we would talk so much, we would there til almost closing, remember that? Yes I do, my little friend. I hated for you to see me in the hospital, but that was part of growing up. You had to face both sides of life and death. I like how you would write letters to me with my little friend.

We shared a lot of picnics, bonfires, feeding your big dogs. Well, you think you are alone and your not. Im looking down at or over your shoulder. Some day, some how we shall meet and who knows when the dead line is and we will have a second chance to share those memories.

In Remembrance of Ruth Heffley 1982

Is it OK to Have a Dream?

I think so. When I was young I had a dream or fantasy about marrying a doctor or lawyer, living in a big house, having children, and living happily ever after. But then I had to face reality and live only one day at a time. I had to take a look at myself and decide which path to take, and heres what I choose.

The fact that I have low self esteem, I'm lonely and unhappy with myself, but why it was the way I was brought up. I was considered a shy and backward person. I have a lot of resentment with my family and friends.

I'd like to dream that one day I may wake up and my problems go away.

I wanted to have a big wedding, to have my whole family in it, both parents walk me down the aisle. This must sound stupid, I wanted to have my panda bear Elizabeth sitting in the pew. But the sad thing is, Elizabeth is no longer living, the other thing is, I know the chances of getting married is zero, the same with having children. I guess I should consider myself lucky having 14 nieces and nephews.

Sometimes it depends on what you eat before you go to bed can make you dream. It can be a happy dream that you don't want to wake up, and then on the other side you can have a scary dream and you would want to wake up quick, and your all sweaty.

I think at one time or another, we dream of marrying a prince charming and having a wonderful life, but that's not necessarily all true.

You can laugh, and I mean laugh at this. When I was little, I wanted to become a nun, I'd never make it now, I've broken a lot of rules. Right now, all I have to do is like who I am today. I'm a good listener, and Ilike to make people happy and do things for people.

Who is This Loretta Person

I guess we can start off by stating her age, I'm 40years old. I'm trying hard to put the pieces of the puzzle of my life together. It all begins when I wake up in the morning, I do a lot of self talk to get up, sometimes I tell myself, "oh shit, I'm still here!" And some days I say, "thank you God."

Some positive things about me is, I enjoy doing things for my friends, caring, good listener, I enjoy working on crafts. I am a shy person.

And there are those negative things about me. I cant says no, I'm afraid of large groups of people, that's one that stops my growth. My weight is another problem. I almost forgot Im able to express my feelings on paper and to some of my friends. But I thank God for my friends and therapists. I have a lot anger and frustration and resentment to express. I found a support system that I turn to.

All I want to do is find piece of mind and happiness with my self, just like my grandmother, contentment. I'm wanting to cry and not think less of myself because I have a lot of hurt and pain built up inside me. I'm a person who has arthritis and a mental disorder and other physical problems. I even shock myself by living this long, considering how many times I thought of suicide. I've been thrown curve balls in my life, I some times think of them as hurdles to jump over.

There's no straight line, its always up and down hills to climb. I know when you reach the age of 40, you cant have children, but I should be happy with all my nieces and nephews.

My life should be in order at some point. All I can say is I'm not afraid to die, I'm afraid to take the risk. There are times life is a challenge, there is so much competition with my family and now I try to accept the fact I'll never measure up to them, it's a losing battle. It's time I realize to think of me as number one first.

Emotion

What's it mean, well I took a minute to look it up in the dictionary and it says : feelings of hate and sorrow, and love. That explains me explains me very well, simple and right to the point, no if and or buts. The feeling of hate I have I can't be myself when I'm around my family members. Lets not use the word hate, its harsh, lets use the word anger. It becomes confusing to be one way with family and another way with friends, doctors, and therapists. Even with them I hide my emotions so they wont never know,

My feeling of sorrow is not being able to accept my grandmothers and my fathers death. The sadness of my own mental illness, dealing the feelings of fear with much of every day situations, fear of crowds, feelings of saying no and be rejected. One big fear is getting fat, fear of trying new things, fear of crying. Another big one is fear of men, fear of not being accepted.

Lets take a look at Love. I love or like helping people. I like being able to work on my cross stitching and give them out for gifts. I enjoy having lunch with my friends. Someday I enjoy riding my bike and other days it's a chore. I enjoy going for walks with Denise.

Sorry bout this, but lets go back to anger. When I want to hurt myself and isolate myself. I never want to hurt people who hurt me. I get angry when too many people depend on me.

I know I'll be happy once I make peace with God, he's the person that accepts and understands me for who I am.

Worry

You know, I could take a bet on it if there was an award given out for the one who worries the most, I'd get it.

Funny how actors get up and want to thank all the people for helping them get the award. Mine would go some thing like this. "I want to thank my mom and dad, my brothers and sisters, also the people I work with, the members of my Tuesday group and I'd never forget my grandmother and some of my relatives and the nieces and nephews and my close friends. Thank you all very much, you don't know what this award means to me, hope to see you all next year."

Others say to me, what do you worry about? Family wise, I worry if my parents have enough money to make it with food, clothes and bills. Same way with my sister and her family, they're making money, but they never have enough, they're always behind with bills. I try to help her out with the kids. I do try to take time to say to myself, "hey, the two of them are working and making more money than me, where does all the worrying get me besides an award, it gets my stomach upset, which causes the nerves to go.

At work, I'm pressured for time and speed, and the employees. I worry about if they have problems. I try to help out when I can, when I can't I still wish I could some how.

17

Even myself, I worry about things like my weight, once in a while money and bills. I've since worked out a budget and it works out. I worry about suicide, that's the way I'll die or I'll get cancer.

And for worrying about my grandmother. I worry when she is sick that she will die. And I know she worries about all of us, she feels she holds us back from doing things or going places.

And for the members of the Tuesday group, they all have some sort of problems that they deal with, which has me worrying.

With work again I worry that I get there on time and make sure I have a clean uniform, neat and clean.

I guess I am supposed to be proud of this award. Part of me is, the other part says "dam it, couldn't you get a different award like the best person award? "On the other hand, I'm just happy to receive just an award. As they say on TV, "Thanks again to everyone who nominated me for this award. Good night and God bless and I hope to see to see all of you next year. Better and stronger than ever.

Do I Believe In Santa Claus?

Im confused, when I was little I believed in Santa because I always wrote Santa Claus a Christmas list, and I would mail it and get a letter back. I would also go to town with my brothers and sisters and we would see Santa and get our pictures taken with Santa Clause.

And on Christmas Eve we would go to church and when we would come home there would be presents under the Christmas tree. We each got three things every year and it seemed as though Santa made sure the girls got a new baby doll and the boys got guns or balls.

Christmas day we would go visit both grandparents and eat dinner. Santa was at their house too, he gave us an envelope with money in it.

As I got older I became confused and started not to believe in Santa Claus because I would see him in a different stores and couldn't figure out how he could be in so many places at one time. And then I would save all my money to buy my mom and dad a Christmas gift, and as the years went by and we all got older we would buy gifts for each other. It was up to my dad to go out and get the Christmas tree and then we would decorate it and my brothers would put up the train set with my dads help and then we would put the presents under the tree.

Who Wants to Live
With Schizoaffective Disorder?

I know I don't want to, but God gave it to me and I have to live with it every day. Its no picnic, its living hell! But there's one good thing about it, I'm not the only one who has Schizoaffective. It can treated, but there is still no cure.

I hear voices telling me to end my life, cut myself, or I see God holding out his hands saying come to me now. Every person is different.

Therapy and medication help calm them down for a little while, but then they come back.

I am a person who has to sign a no harm contract every month, sometimes week to week, because Im not sure if I am going to live. I get my medicine on a weekly basis, so I don't overdose. I'm a very unhappy person with Schizoaffective, but I'm still hanging on along with the others who have Schizoaffective. I couldn't do it without my whole support system and most important . . . God!

Life

Sometimes, I think of life as a joke and there are times when I look at life seriously. What I mean is some days I get and say to myself, "shit you made it another night." And yet when I've been sick and felt like I was dying, I was scared to death. There are days that I felt helpless and out of control. I just cant get a good a grip of myself until I stop and say hang in there and you'll be okay.

One day I take serious is my birthday. People don't understand, what its like to make it another year, and what it was just to make it another year on my job. That was a big accomplishment for me, considering I was ready to quit a few days after I started. I've learned that other people have problems like me, but handle them different. I understand life has its ups and downs, you just have to accept it, as someone once said to me, "go with the flow."

Even though there's game called life, you cant play with your own life that way. When you think of it, life is what you make it, you have control.

I still feel there will be a day, I'll be happy where I am at. It may not be today or tomorrow, but I know someday I'll be free and I'll just be me.

Look Into the Mirror

I take a good long look into the mirror and what do I see? I see a girl, no I take that back, a young woman who is 43 years old and very unhappy with her life.

She seldom smiles, she feels she's being treated like a ginney pig. A pill for this a pill for that. What's good for one thing, isn't good for something else.

She's a kind and caring person, honest, open minded, loveable, she wants to be treated with respect, that's just a few to name.

She leads a confusing life when she's around her family. She doesn't allow them to them to see her anger or depression. When she's with friends, she lets the real person show herself.

This woman finds herself happy when she's doing crafts, being around her friends and helping others. This woman is unhappy and depressed when she is being taken advantage of, used and abused, and when hearing voices and knowing she is going to die soon. Which she is not afraid of. She depends mostly on herself and some of her support system. She enjoys being alone sometimes, not having to answer to anyone, being her own boss.

Have you given up on guessing who this person is? Okay, I'll tell you . . . its me, Loretta Knapp. Depressed and ready to die!

Elizabeth Geiser
1819-1990

My Grandmother

First of all her name is Elizabeth. She was the best and number one grandmother in the whole wide world. As I recall when I was a child and my family would go visit my grandparents, they had a big yard and some toys for us to play with but before we would go home we had to clean up.

As my grandmother got older she wasn't able to clean her house so my sister and I took turns on weekends to help her, she paid us $5.00. She made cakes from scratch, she never used a mixer. I was amazed how she mixed up her cakes. She seldom got angry, she had a regular schedule. Monday was her wash day, Tuesday was ironing. I don't remember Wednesday or Thursday, but Friday was hair day, Saturday was cleaning and Sunday was church day.

My grandmother was a nice and caring woman, she'd give you her last dollar.

She always wore dresses, she didn't own a pair of pants. She crochet afghans in the winter and lap covers and pillow covers in the summer. She suffered from arthritis in her hands, shoulders, and knees.

When she got older our family moved in with our grandparents. My grandmother needed help going up and down stairs. Between my sisters and me and my mom, we took turns. As time went on, she was gradually going down hill. She then needed help getting dressed and bathed, this only brought me and my grandmother closer.

She prayed a lot not only for herself, but for her family. She said rosemary every night before she went to sleep. When she wasn't able to go to church, the priest came to the house every first Friday of the month.

Then came the time when she was confined to her room, we tried to make her a comfortable as possible. She had a TV, recliner chair, a big bed, and a potty chair. She no longer wore dresses due to her arthritis, she wore night gowns. We had to take a tub of water up her to her room to bath her. I recall on holidays, I'd take a plate of food up to her and eat with her so she wasn't alone. She would get the readers digest and I'd always read the laughter is the best medicine. We would laugh. On Sundays, in the after noon we would watch a movie and both fall asleep and wake up before its over. My grandmothers mind was clear up to the end.

I remember there were days when my grandmother didn't understand why God didn't take her. My grandmother was a kind hearted, lovable, caring, crafty, honest, and all that good stuff. My grandmother and I shared a lot of good times together.

I miss her very much. I make it a point to visit her on her birthday and anniversary of her death. I take a rose with me and we have a little talk.

My grandmother had four sons and one daughter. My uncle took care of her finances, but as for taking care of grandmother, that was up to mom and I and my sister.

My mom and I take care of the graves and plant flowers to make it look nice. I'm sure she likes them.

My grandmother turned 95 on march 20th, and died April 5th. She did suffer, she had shingles. But no matter what, it didn't take the pain away from me. She was loved and well liked by everyone and sadly missed.

In Remembrance of Elizabeth Geiser 1990
Born 1895

Who Am I

Think, think, think, That's what Winnie the Pooh says. I'm a 43 yeah old lady or woman, whatever. Living with a mental illness, but seeking help for it. Scott told me its Satan doing it and I should shout, I fear that some day Satan's going to win. I would pray every day that my depression would let up.

I admit, I am a happy person when I am playing with my nieces and nephews.

I like being independent, by living on my own. I don't have to answer to anyone. I can come and go as I please. Im a person who thinks of other people, to help when I can. I like to work on my cross stitch and give them away as gifts. I like having lunch with Shirley once a week.

I wish could be my self around my family and friends. I show my true feelings in group and therapists, its hard on me. I'm over weight, but working on it. I'm a person who has a negative outlook on life and my self, but with the help of therapy my attitude about myself is getting better. Like I'm a good listener, caring person, kind hearted, understanding, honest, open minded, gifted, clean, dependable, friendly, likeable. Looking at all this, Im not such a bad person.

But why would a person like me want to end her life? For one, I'm tired of fighting the voices, jumping over hurdles, running into road blocks. I wouldn't give my illness to anyone I want to be a happy person, I want to be accepted for who I am. I guess what Im trying to say is, Im a 43 old woman who has some growing to do and risks to take. But better yet, just to be myself.

Who Am I

Im still 43, but lost for words. I just lost my two best friends. I feel left alone, don't know where to turn. Since I was a child, I always felt life wasn't for me, and now as an adult I still feel the same way.

I have a weight problem and I got that from my mother. I have arthritis in my hands and knees, which I inherited from my grandmother and mother. I suffer with depression and anxiety and schizophrenia for several years and being treated for it. I have a kitten named Tiger, she keeps me company. I do yell at her at times, but she knows when Im not feeling well, and comforts me.

One thing that makes me happy is when I am around my nieces and nephews. I enjoy watching Tv, doing crafts, enjoy helping others. I am a good listener. I never knew love was so hard to get.

I like music like Anne Murray, John Denver, Bee Gees, Neil Diamond, Barry Manalow, Simon and Garfunkle, and Bobby Goldsburg. People tell me I'm not a bad person, some days I find that hard to believe. Part of me knows, I am kind and caring, understanding, good listener, honest open minded, shy, gifted person

For me, life is one struggle after another. I jump over one hurdle and there's another one standing right there. I am an unhappy person.

Who Am I

To begin, im 43 soon to be 44 on August 23 (2002). I have physical, emotional, and mental problems. I come from a family of seven, and out of the seven, I'm the black sheep of the family.

I feel like a door mat because every one walks over me and takes advantage of me.

I'm a people pleaser, afraid to say no fear of being rejected. I live on my own, I enjoy the fact that I can get up when I want to, eat when I want to. I guess what I am trying to say is, I don't have to answer to anyone. I keep myself clean. I find myself as a caring, honest, open minded, shy, gifted, kindhearted person. I enjoy being around my nieces and nephews. I also enjoy doing crafts like cross stitching and giving them a way for a gift. I'm afraid to show my feelings. My favorite colors are red and blue. Why?? Because they are strong colors. My favorite food is pizza with extra cheese. But you see, I'm 43 and don't want to live.

I'm a confused and troubled woman. When I am with my family, I am a different person. And when I around my support they see the real me.

Feelings

Feelings, lets face it, we all have feelings of some sort. Take time and think, for me I have feelings of happiness. Surprised ya!

That's when I'm with my little nieces and nephews or when I'm with my friend Gale. She has a way of making me laugh.

I have feelings of sadness when my family hurts me which brings tears that I cry. When I think of my dad and grandma, and Shirley, they understood me and shared some of my good times together. I'm sad when Gales not feeling well. There's a feeling of pain right now where I had back surgery, when my knee hurts me. Or when I see someone else in pain.

There's a feeling of loneliness and grieving that comes from like missing my dad, grandma and Shirley.

There's also a feeling of caring and thoughtfulness. I'm always willing to help out when I can and do things for others.

I've left the last feeling of suicide That always enters my mind, I think if I ended my life I'd have peace of mind and so would others.

Feelings of hope that things will work out and then there's the opposite, hopelessness, where things will never change. Feeling of helpless, feelings of anger. So lets look back, I think I covered all the feelings. Happiness, sadness, pain, loneliness, grieving, caring, helpful, thoughtfulness, suicide, peace of mind, and guilt.

My Own Experience With Mental Illness

My own experience, looking at me on the out side, I look normal. But what really counts is how I feel on the inside. I've been diagnosed with Schitzo effective.

Its hard and becomes complicated when you don't have family support and your fighting for your life. What I mean is the voices and the hallucinations, when they are telling you to cut your self, take all your medications, and dealing with the mood swings . . . the highs and the lows.

But now I'm trying to lead as much of a normal life as possible. I live on my own, I pay my own bills, continue therapy, and take my medications, even though I only keep a week supply at a time. Things I enjoy doing are, doing cross stitch, watching TV, and playing with my cat Tiger. She is what I think brought me out of my depression.

Due to my illness, I don't like being around crowds of people. I think I'm a kind, caring, and friendly person. So I feel I may be a little different from others, but I've been dealing with it for many years, and accepting it myself. I always knew there was something wrong, but I didn't know what it was. Now that I know it, makes it easier to understand and cope. Each day I strive to stay alive.

What Makes Loretta Special

Lets see, for one there's only one of me, thank God for that. I don't think God or family could handle two of me.

The other thing is, my name is not a popular one. That depresses me cause I can never find my name anywhere.

Loretta had a tough up bringing, didn't have much of a childhood. I matured at an early age, which didn't help any.

I was a shy backwards person. I was always wanting to run a way from home.

But I think what makes me special is I'm a kind hearted, caring person, likeable, friendly, easy to get along with, honest, open minded, good listener, clean, and work on crafts and always giving them away. I enjoy being around my nieces and nephews, and they like me. I live on my own, which makes me happy. I work hard at pleasing my family and other people. I'm a sensitive person. I have a cat named Tiger that keeps me on my toes.

I guess what I'm trying to say is, Loretta is a special person, not only to herself, but to other people too. She has to believe in herself.

What's In a Smile

A smile on your face can cheer someone up, it can also brighten some ones day!

I find when I'm walking and nod my head and give a friendly have a good day, or a hello, or just a smile . . . they smile back.

For me a smile on my face can mean Im feeling good, I'm happy, I want to be around people, I want to do things. I enjoy walking, arts and crafts, helping other people, being around Tiger, my cat, taking pictures, and doing thing with my family.

A smile can be comforting to some one who is sick.

When the sun comes out, most of us smile. I know I do even for a little while. So you see, a smile can mean a lot of things.

Its 3:00 am and I am writing this. Tiger is pacing the floor saying we should be in bed sleeping, but I am just smiling to clear me head.

My problem is I don't smile enough. What do you think?

So next time you see some one, give them a smile and see what happens. It wont hurt giving it a try.

How Do People See Me

This is a serious question. People look at me as a strong and brave person. I'm caring, kind, likeable, trusting, honest, friendly, and open minded. They're right about that some of it. Being brave, at one time I was, but I cant be brave anymore. It's just not my surgery, its being around men, being around crowds, asking for help, and depending people after my surgery. The only ones that see me break down are Pat, Luanne, Denise, crisis, and Tiger.

North Fork Dam

Special Place

I sit here as the sun bears down on my face, shines on the leaves as I watch them change into beautiful colors like red, yellow and a few green ones left on the tree branch. The empty tree limbs are still.

And then there's water, I gaze down at it as it clear water flows down the stream. It's a peaceful place. God made it for someone like me who has problems and just wants to escape from it all. Its quiet and no one bothers you. Your at peace and tranquility, you can use your imagination.

I don't share this place to too many people, because its my special place. And I think God was thinking of me when he made this place. So, THANK YOU GOD!

Dreams

We all have dreams growing up. Think about it, it probably happened when you were in 2nd grade. I know little boys want to grow up and be just like their dads, or become a doctor, a fireman, or a police man. That's just to name a few.

Now little girls are different. They usually want to grow up to be like their moms. It may be a nurse, secretary, a beautician, or like me. I wanted to be like my mom, a house wife. I wanted to grow up, get married, raise a family. My husband would have a good paying job, so I can stay home and run the house. Like do the cleaning, cooking, washing clothes, and taking good care of my children and husband and keeping them happy.

But that was only a dream and it got shattered. My dream will never come alive, while others may come true. It's okay to have a dream.

Turkey Trot Race

Here it is turkey time again. That means on Thanksgiving Day they hold a turkey trot race. One year I entered the race, mind you I was no young turkey, I wasn't real old either. I recall that day very well, I started out good, but then I slowed down. I gradually was falling behind more and more.

There was two other turkeys with me in this race, we were so far behind we ended up making up our own trail. We did finish the race, the funny thing we never got caught to make it for somebody's turkey dinner.

My Head

My head used to lean over to the side now its sits up straight. You may ask why did it lean over?

It had to do with my childhood. Growing up wasn't so easy. I had many rough times, but I bounced back.

When I was at the age to seek out help or attention for my problems, I started to get better. Talking to a therapists, going to group, taking my medication, hanging around my support system, put my head straight.

You see, in 2003 I had back surgery against my whole family's wishes. Then in the year 2005 I had a hysterectomy. Now I have arthritis in both my knees.

I've had my share of problems, but I'll try to keep my head straight up, because when and if my head would fall down I would be in trouble.

Easter

You can look at it in two ways. One way it is a sad time, because that's when Jesus died on the cross for us. But he had suffered for forty days. It rained forty days and forty nights. Jesus had the apostles with him.

When Jesus carried the cross, he fell three times and one of the other apostles took the cross for him for a while. But I remember so very well when Jesus was nailed to the cross and put up to die. He said "Father forgive them, for they do not know what they have done", and then he died. Second way you can look at Easter is, you go to church, you come home and get your Easter basket full of candy and eggs. Then you have an Easter dinner and Easter egg hunt. Girls usually get new dresses and shoes and hats for Easter. Easter can be a fun time.

Hear Voices

Hearing voices isn't a pleasant thing to live with. Imagine yourself hearing voices day and night, its enough to drive you crazy. I can speak for myself, my name is Loretta Knapp and I have been hearing voices for a number of years. Its treatable but there's not a cure. I'm being treated for them with medication and other coping skills, such as calling a friend, working on cross stitch, watching TV, talking to my therapists or counselors, or play with my cat, tell them to go to hell, get out of here, leave me alone, and I even try to pray the rosemary. Sometimes it works and sometimes it doesn't, it depends on my stress level.

The voices I hear are always telling me to harm myself, to cut my stomach or my arms, never to hurt any one else. They also say times running out and be not afraid. I some times hear an organ playing. I also see God holding out his hands saying come to me.

Take time out of your day and imagine yourself having to live with the voices, its not pleasant, is it. I wouldn't want any one to go through what I am experiencing.

Life isn't easy for me. I take one day at a time, sometimes minute to minute. I know there are other people out there experiencing the same thing as I am and it's not a piece of cake for them either. They just deal with it in other ways. Some do commit suicide and that's what I'm afraid is going to happen to me.

Pain

There are many different types of pain. There are paper cuts pain, there are pains from scrape of a knee when you were a child me, I had back surgery. Talk about a pain that's really painful. Any kind of surgery is painful. A broken leg or arm.

Pain can some harsh words spoken between friends. I imagine a baby drinking a bottle too fast and then being filled with gas.

Another type of pain is the loss of a loved one, grieving.

You may think this is crazy, but Christ had pain when he was nailed to the cross and put up to die. And what did he say . . . "Father forgive them for they do not know what they have done."

When we have pain we call the doctors and he or she prescribes medicine.

To Grow

In order for me to grow there are certain steps I must take.

1. Get plenty of water.
2. Feed me some miracle grow and place me near the window, So I can get plenty of sun.
3. Now you can watch me blossom in to somebody I want to be, but don't forget to feed me from time to time.

And don't over feed me for I shall die and have no future.

LOVE
Incontrol
MAXINE
Secure
CAROLE
FRAN
Delores
HAPPY
THATS
LIFE
KIND Hearted
DREAMS
PAIN
ANGER
FAMILY
FRIENDS

Bear Puzzle

Here is a puzzle made very carefully and put together by me. It took time and patience, it wasn't easy as doing a child's puzzle and yet when I was little they were still hard to put together, but the puzzle I'm putting together is an adult puzzle.

I'm piecing parts of my life together. First I had to select the picture that wasn't difficult. I chose the panda bear. That is one animal I love. I collect them. I'm almost like them, hard to mate.

Then I had to chose the words and figure out what word goes where, what color to use for each. The words I have to pick out deal with my feelings of what I keep inside of me and the others what I express on the outside.

The words family and friends I've done in dark colors. I put them on the border of the puzzle, with out my family and the little friends I have, they've helped me through the good times and bad times. My friends always gave me an ear to listen to my problems. They helped me to see things a little different. Instead of trying to help me end my life, they helped me to continue on.

One thing they always ended things by saying is, "that's life". I left that piece of the puzzle last to put in later, I'll tell you why. Without the help of my friends I'd be standing still, but instead they taught me to move on and stand tall.

The words secure, Love, dreams, anger, pain, happy, along with the others. These are all things we deal with as a part of our daily lives. On bad days I have hard time dealing with the pain and hurt, which causes me more frustration.

I have a hard time thinking of the good things about me: kindhearted, loving, hard worker, and always willing to help others out even though sometimes I cant even help myself. But as Maxine and others would say again, that's life, its all a part of growing up and everyone goes through the things I go through. They just have a different way of dealing with them.

Another example is my weight for me to lose. I have to gain control and stay in control until I lose enough and block out what others say. I have nothing against heavy people. I'm just a person who strives to be thin.

The words I put on the border are all strong words. I saved the words "that's life' to put in last mainly because again the words I picked out for this puzzle deal with my life. Every time I talk to my friends, they ended things by saying, that's life. It wasn't the easiest piece to put in because sometimes I can't accept these things as part of my life.

Putting this puzzle together wasn't easy, but again, nothing ever is. But it was a challenge for me

Please do keep in mind that the puzzle is made up of one and only one person. All the characteristics are, guess who? This puzzle is me. What do you think?

My Journey of Recovery

Here I am, 47 years old, I look up, I look down, I look side to side for some sense of direction. Til one day when I was 18 years and I went counseling. I had dreams, but they were shattered. I wanted to get married and have children, but I know that's not going to happen.

I have a special place to go in the summer and fall where I take a picnic lunch and watch the water flow and the leaves change color. In the winter, I just envision what its like.

I've had some pretty rough times growing up in my child hood and as an adult. Nobody knows how many hurdles I've had to jump over one after another to get where I am at today. Many of the times I wanted to give up and let the ship sink. I'd cry out for help from my support team. If I didn't have the them I wouldn't be standing here today.

Even now, I still sign a no harm contract every month with Luann, my caseworker. Sometimes I sign them week to week. They mean a lot to me. I have to take it day by day, minute by minute. Life isn't easy for me. People have told me that I do not know what it is like to have fun, but I am learning with my friends.

Every night before I go to bed, I thank God for giving me another day to live, and most of all I thank him for giving me a support system. Which helps me through tough times.

It took me a long time to find that support system and to place my trust in these people (Luann, Pat, Janice, Trish, and Gale). They've given me a reason to live and they're helping me with my depression. I'm on a long and narrow road to recovery. When I am with my support system, I can be myself and continue to grow and live independently. I look forward to the future.

I won $100.00 for this recovery story.

Tiger, My Cat

Tiger

What can I say about Tiger? First of all, she was trouble when I first got her. I received her from Jane, a lady at Cambria County MHMR. She was two or three months old, I cant really recall. She was trouble the first day I brought he home. I had a big box blocking off the living room to the kitchen. I showed her where the liter box was and the cat food was and all. So I go lay down and I hear a thump. It was Tiger, she jumped over the box and came into the living room and meowed at me. I didn't know what to do, I just had to laugh.

When she was old enough to get fixed, I had it done. She was a funny kitten. She had a ball and would take it up the steps and let it bounce back down the steps at 2 a.m. in the morning. Thank God I didn't have neighbors. Next thing she would do is when I'd take a bath she would sit at the rim of the tub and bat at the bubbles, until one night she fell into the tub. I'm not done yet. I'd be riding my exercise bike and she'd jump up and wrap herself around my neck and watch me ride my bike. When I'd get off, I'd have to stoop down and then she'd jump down.

When she was two years old, I decided to give her a treat. Boy was that a mistake. I gave her Bumblebee tuna fish. Now she wakes me up at 1:30 or 2:30 in the morning for tuna fish. At that same age she learned to turn the stereo on and watch the record go around. Don't get me wrong, I love Tiger, she's like a baby to me. At age three, I don't know what she'll be like.

I tell her I love her many times throughout the day. I sometimes fall asleep on the couch, and when I wake up Tiger is on me. Tiger has helped me when I'm depressed or sick. Just reecently, I found that she is very protective over me. She also sleeps with me at night. That was the terrible twos. I don't know if I'm up to see the threes.

Things are bad, when I leave the house I leave a light and radio on. On hot days I let the fan on. Now tell me, would a normal person do that for a cat? But I look at it this way, she's been there for me through some tough times. She makes me laugh when I am depressed. She is there when no one else is. She's my baby! What can I say . . . . I love her.

I Am Poem

I'm a shy person, but easy to get along with.

I'm a friendly person, and kind hearted and trustworthy, just who I am.

I'm an overweight person, but that's okay. That's something I'm working on each day.

I like to write and someday I hope to write a book.

I like it at my apartment. Its quiet and I can play with my cat.

I look for guidance and support for my problems, but that don't make me weak.

I am what God made me.

What it Feels Like to be in Recovery

It feels like you're your on the highest mountain or cloud. But it means you reach your goal. For me, it was hard and difficult at times to work on my goal, but with the help of my support team, they kept me going

Sure I had some relapses, but I never let it show. I know when I achieve my goal it will be a new beginning. Its going to be like opening a new can of worms, as some would say. It will be scary at first, but once I start I'll be okay. I'll miss my support team, but I'll keep in touch. Being in recovery is a good thing.

Stop and just take a few minutes to have a laugh here or there. Lets go back to when you were say maybe at the age of 6 or 7 and you and your friend were out for a walk and you come across a lucky stone.

So you each decide to pick one up, of course we start arguing whose is bigger, but then we both put our heads together and realize that their both shaped different. Then I throw my stone on the ground and kick it and my friend did the same thing trying to see who's went further.

We come across a river and we both look at each other and took the last look at our stones and throw the stone in the river. It splashes and that was the last of our lucky stone.

Life

Lets take a look at the word life and what it means to me. For one, I believe I take life too serious. And for another, obviously I don't spend time putting much fun in my life. Don't get me wrong, I have fun with my friend Gale and my nieces and nephews, and now June my peer specialist. I have fun teasing Jason with the snack cart.

I spend a lot of time praying that I make it through the day and sometimes through the night. Some how God pulls me through. And from time to time I write stories, which I hope that one day God can help me write a book. Some one once said life is a bowl full of cherries. I think they're wrong. Some one else said life is a ray full of sun shine. I'm not sure about that one.

Life starts when you get out of bed and say Good morning God and the sun is out and end with the saying goodnight God along with the moon and stars. And thank Him for helping me get through the struggles and jumping over the hurdles again today. Amen.

How has Pat Hydock Helped Me

I stand here amongst you 200 people to talk about Pat.

For one, she has given me hope when I didn't think I was going to make it. She has also given me courage to move on.

And one big one in life, when I was suicidal and felt the world was crashing down, Pat never gave up on me. She would have me sign a no harm contract. I believe in them and Pat holds me to them.

It took some time for Pat to convince me its okay to cry. Now I know, soon as I get into her office and before the door shuts, the tears start coming. Pat has been a good support. She has one thing that she can make me laugh when I'm having a bad day, and that's green polka dotted pajamas.

Pat gives guidance and some how always steers me in the right direction by the end of my appointment. Pat is a good person and deserves recognition for it.

She goes above and beyond her limitation. I've been seeing Pat for several years and I place my trust and faith in her. Pat puts all she got into her job, so I hope her co workers appreciate it. She deserves a round of applause.

Taking a Walk

One day I woke up and decided to take a morning stroll, I ended up ina little town Middle Taylor. It consisted of a Lutheran Church and a bank that was open from 8am to 4pm. As I was going by I passed up two videos stores and another Dollar general store. When I got closer to the town there was another church and on the opposite side of the street was Sheryl's Pet store.

One thing I did take notice to, that there was only one Ambulance Service Station. I also recall, one of my class mates lived in a trailer some where. Still going along on my right, I saw a laugh and learn day care center, which will help me out when I go home and tell my friend.

Well, its getting late and the gas tank is running low and I'm hungry and the sun is going down, but I had a nice enjoyable day.

Many of bridges I've crossed over where sometimes the river banks were high, but somehow I get across them. When I was down and lost my faith on God, some how he helps carry me over that bridge. There always seems along the way that there was another bridge to cross.

Each time I cross the bridge its supposed to make me stronger, but some how it doesn't. My support system would praise me and say you made it through another day and be thankful.

I think my body and mind are stronger than what I give my self credit for, I don't know, what do you think?

Next time I cross the bridge I'm going to take my time and put my feet in the hands of God.

On The Road To Recovery

On the road to recovery doesn't happen over night. It takes time and patience and guidance and support. It takes one day at a time, for me sometimes its minute to minute.

Have you ever heard of taking peep peep steps? One therapists told me to try that and it works.

It was some what of a challenge. You learn to grow you build up your self esteem and you learn about yourself. Over the years I've come out of my shell. I wouldn't have been able to do that with out the help of Pat Hydock, Psych rehab, and my best friends Gale and Debbie, plus a little help from my family.

I still suffer with depression and hearing voices, but I'm learning to cope. I think that's what recovery is all about, learning to manage your systems, build support, grow, and move on and still learn about yourself.

Special Person

There's a special person who's meant very much to me. She is my second cousin to me and she's only 85 years old. Her name is Anna Mary Courtney. She's out going, open minded, honest, caring, loving, friendly, good listener, and helpful. For 85, she still drives, goes exercising, swimming classes. She has a strong belief in God and very religious. She has her aches and pains, but never complains. She lives by herself and maintains a house. She has a son and two daughter who mean a lot to her. They are a close family and help their mother when she needs it. She is there for me when I need to talk to her. She gives me guidance when I need it and points me in the right direction.

Soon to be 50 years old

Soon to be 50 and everything looks so gray right now, how come? I don't know. Maybe its because its how they say it, it's the BIG 50.

I guess maybe its time to take a stroll down memory lane and take a look at what I've accomplished in my past years.

Well taking a step back when I graduated from high school, I reached out for psychiatric help as soon as possible and yes I am not ashamed to admit it. I had it rough for a while. I was still living at home and lived on welfare. Then my psychologists suggested I go to the Hiram G Andrews center. I took up a cooking course for two years. I learned a lot. While doing that I took up jogging. I was running 5 1/2 miles a day. I ran in some races mainly for a charity. I did come in second place in one. In the mean time I was still getting counseling and put on medicine. I also spent two weeks before Hiram G Andrews, in the hospital, that was uncalled for because the person I was seeing lost her license.

In between I got a job a t Dunkin doughnuts for 6 months and lost that job and got a job at McDonalds for 5 ½ years. I moved out on my own at the age of 19. I was the grill person and did many other jobs there. But keep in mind, every year my birthday came up I wanted to end my life. After I left McDonalds, I went to Penelec and worked in the canteen as a dishwasher, that was the turning point.

I got real sick and had to quit my job and ended up on social security and SSI. While working a t McDonalds, I met a man and got engaged. It turned out he did some mean stuff to me and I broke off the engagement. From then on I thought all men were dirty and I was afraid of them.

I don't mean to repeat myself, but when I got sick and lost my job, I ended up spending time at my mom and dads because I couldn't take care of myself at that time. I forgot my grandmother passed away while I was working at the Penelec, and I didn't have a chance to say good bye, only at the funeral home. I had some resentment. Oh well, when I went back to my apartment I just laid around. Then one day my dad asked me if I wanted to go for a walk and get coffee, so I did. We did that a couple times a week and soon I was able to take care of myself and make decisions.

I was seeing a therapist, Claire Garber. I only saw her for a short time because she got sick with cancer and never came back. Then there was sandy Mack, I saw her for a short time then Maxine Kane suggested I start going to Partial, that's where I met a woman named Pat Hydock. She was very nice to me. I was scared, I recall my first day there, I cried. Pat took me in her office and we talked. I also met a case worker. In Partial, I learned about coping skills, depression, current events, social skills and even learned how to laugh. The groups were run by different case workers. I was there for 3 years. While there I became friendly with a lady named Shirley. We became real close friends, because after I left partial, I would still meet Shirley for lunch.

While I was in Partial, my dad passed away. I remember that day so clear as if it were today. I went to other groups after partial like grieving, stress management, and I saw a counselor Anne. After she left we became friends.

Shirley and I did a lot of things together until she became ill. I took her for therapy. We would go to lunch and spend time together. She went down hill fast. I came home one evening and called her. Someone strange answered the phone, then her close friend Patty got on the phone and told me Shirley had died. I was in shock! It was up to Patty and I to make the final arrangements. Shirley had made them all, but we had to finalize them. She left Patty with the trailer house, which was big. She left both of us a ring, and she also gave me a lot of money, that I was taken off my Social Security and SSI. I only had a few months to spend it and show what the money was used for. I did buy a lot of new stuff, like a new TV and entertainment center, a stereo system. Went to my uncles birthday party and slept in a hotel with my brother and his wife and my mom went. I paid for the food, gas, and hotel. I got new clothes and some other stuff. I wasn't allowed to give donations to a church or organizations. I got a car. When it came down to it, I was a very unhappy person. I was depressed and cried a lot. My uncle helped me out with a lot of the legal stuff. I was happy for that.

I see Pat Hydock, I know she didn't know what to do with me, but she kept having me sign a no harm contract. I went into isolation and was depressed. Then one day I decide to volunteer at the Atrium Manor. I worked there for a couple of months and then had to stop because of my back.

Finally, my family doctor told me to get a cane and then she sent me to Dr. Haque. They put me through a series of tests and then he said surgery was the only solution. My family was against the surgery. I went a head and did it anyways and he put a steel rod in my back and diffused two disks. I went through a lot. I'll never forget Father James meeting me at the hospital at 5:30 am and gave me a blessing. That was in 2002. The surgery went great. I had to go to therapy and wear a back brace. I had a nurse come every other day and shower me and take care of me. My mom washed my clothes and changed my bandage on my back the days the nurse didn't come. I thank her very much. LuAnne, my case manager came to visit me just about every day on her lunch break. She was very nice and still is. She reads all my medical papers that I don't understand.

Well I had another medical problem with my period ever since I stared at the age of ten or eleven. It was terrible. I had what they call PMS syndrome. I don't give a dam what they called it, I don't want it. Finally when I was in my forties convinced them to give me a hysterectomy, thaty happened in the year 2005. Sister Carol jean helped out with that part, they finally listened to her.

Sister Carol Jean and I had many talks and went for walks and had coffee together until she had an aneurism to the brain which affected her memory. They had to put her in a home. I haven't seen or talked to her in a long time. I miss her very much.

When I turned 45, Luanne suggested I go to psych rehab, so I agreed. I met a lot of people there. The support system is good. When you need to talk to staff, they make the time for you. When I turned between the ages of 46 to 47 I started to show signs of menopause. Its hard to deal with the hot flashes, mood swings, I'm just having a hard time with it. On August 23rd, I will turn 50 years old. I'm not looking forward to it, I want to end my life. I don't even want to see that day. I want to go peacefully.

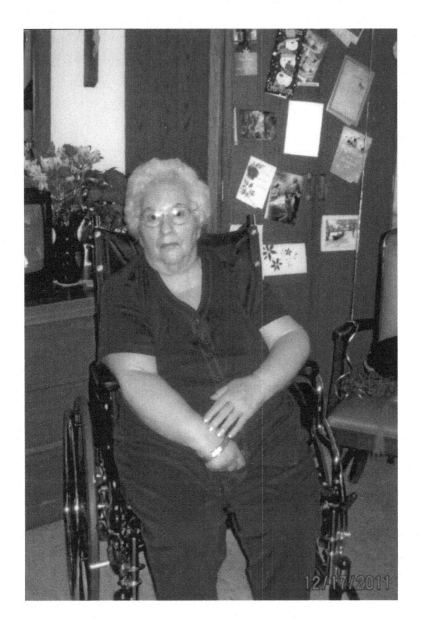

My Mother

My Mother

What can I say about my mother? Well, for one she didn't make my life easy. She tried to raise seven children and keep every one of them happy. Imagine trying to do that?

All I wanted from my mom was love and I found that hard to get. I know I wasn't an angel and I had problems. I was different from the other six children, I was a loner and felt rejected.

My mom had it tough. After most of us kids were grown up she ended taking care of her own mother, which was tough, but she managed it well with the help of me and my sister Barb.

Still I was looking for my moms love, And I had a hard time showing her love too. So it went both ways.

Now she's in a nursing home and I'll never get that love. So its time for me to show and give her all the love she needs now. I do love her very much and always will no matter what til the end. She someone I'll always treasure because she is very special to me and holds a special place in my heart.

Last . . . Did Loretta Have Fun In Her Life?

Sure I did have some fun, it was far and in in between. When I was young and growing up, on Saturday nights my dad would take turns taking one of us kids to church. And when it was my turn, I behaved. We would go to the club, and I would have cherry pop and chips. Then we would go home of course, and my dad would have his beer.

As I grew up my grandmother needed help cleaning her house. So, between me and my sister Barb, we took turns on weekends to help clean the house. The fun part was watching my grandmother make a cake. She would hold the bowl in her arm and mix it with a wooden spoon in her other hand.

Holidays were fun also. Gathering at my grandparents house eating and seeing all the relatives. But what was also exciting was seeing my grandfathers train set.

I started writing stories when I was young. I enjoyed jogging and running in races, like the ones with children with learning disabilities, turkey trot and walking for alszymers. I did some volunteering at my church when I was young I helped count the Sunday collection. The churches name was Saint Columbia. I worked there with my friends Karen, Connie, Audrey, Paul and the secretary Carol. They then closed that church down and I am now volunteering at Saint John Gualbert. I stuff the envelopes for the shut ins. I have a chance here to talk to Maria and Irene. I used to enjoy baking, but since ive been sick I no longer enjoy it. I also volunteered for special Olympics at the Atrium Manor for a short time. I also volunteered for New Day, which I enjoyed.

I enjoyed spending time with my mom on Sundays when the two of us would go up to my sisters Barbs for dinner. I'd take the vegetables and my mom would take the dessert. It was nice seeing my nieces and nephews. My sister would also have picnics and invite us up. I enjoyed that also.

I have a friend Debbie, I call once a week or she calls me. I have a friend June, I talk to a couple times a week. I have a friend Gale, she calls me "silver foxxette #1". We talk every day and do things together. My mom and I did things together when she was able to, but now she's in a nursing home.

And so you see, I did have some fun.

Dear Lord,

I'm asking for your help to get me on the right track. I made a wrong turn along my journey. I made a left turn instead of a right. I wasn't sure this morning, should I get out of the left side of the bed or the right side. Help me to put theses feelings in the right place. Sure, I made mistakes, everyone makes mistakes.

My journey in life has made more lefts than rights. But that's okay, nobody's perfect. I might be late, but the best thing to do is ask someone for directions and get gas, and stop and eat. All of that should give me peace of mind, which is hard for me to find. I've made a right turn by seeing Pat Hydok, going to psyche rehab, staying with a support system, taking my medication. All that has got me on my journey to recovery, as I made a right turn. When I fall, I just pick my self up and dust my self off and start all over again.

GOD BLESS ALL WHO TAKE THIS JOURNEY

Loretta

Take care of <u>yourself first.</u>
Your just as important as anyone else.
Laughter is the Best medicine.
When you laugh the whole world will laugh <u>with </u>you, cry and they cry
    with you.
You're a <u>good </u>person!
<u>Don't</u> be afraid to ask for help when you <u>need</u> to
Loretta . . . .
Your NOT a bad person.